JOSEPH ROSA

design series[1]

SAN FRANCISCO MUSEUM OF MODERN ART

SFMOMA design series

ROY IS THE FIRST IN A SERIES OF EXHIBITIONS AND ACCOMPANYING PUBLICATIONS
INTENDED TO HIGHLIGHT THE WORK OF ARCHITECTS, GRAPHIC DESIGNERS, AND
INDUSTRIAL DESIGNERS AT THE FOREFRONT OF THEIR RESPECTIVE DISCIPLINES. THIS
VOLUME IS PUBLISHED ON THE OCCASION OF THE EXHIBITION ROY/DESIGN SERIES 1,
ORGANIZED BY JOSEPH ROSA AT THE SAN FRANCISCO MUSEUM OF MODERN ART
AND ON VIEW FROM APRIL 19 TO SEPTEMBER 7, 2003.

ROY/design series 1 is organized by the San Francisco Museum of
Modern Art. Generous support for this exhibition has been provided
by an anonymous donor.

The San Francisco Museum of Modern Art is a private, not-for-profit
institution supported by its members, individual contributors to Donor
Circle, corporate and foundation support, federal and state government
grants, and admission revenues. Annual programming is sustained
through the generosity of Grants for the Arts/San Francisco Hotel
Tax Fund and The James Irvine Foundation.

Acting Director of Publications: Chad Coerver
Editor: Karen A. Levine
Designer: Lia Tjandra
Printing: Celeste McMullin, the Printcess/Hemlock Printers
Printed and bound in Canada

Cover image: Wind River Lodge, Chugach mountain range, 2001–, perspective
Inside cover: Noah, New York, 2001–, detail of optical fiber braid
All images courtesy of ROY with the following exceptions: page 11,
reproduced by permission of Barbara and Julian Neski; pages 12 and 37,
photographic material courtesy of Richard Misrach. The photograph
of subWave was taken by Gernot Riether

Library of Congress Cataloging-in-Publication Data

Rosa, Joseph.
    Roy : design series 1 / Joseph Rosa.
        p. cm.—(SFMOMA design series ; 1)
"This catalogue is published by the San Francisco Museum of Modern Art
on the occasion of the exhibition ROY/design series 1, organized by
Joseph Rosa at the San Francisco Museum of Modern Art and on view
from April 19 to September 7, 2003."
    Includes bibliographical references.
    ISBN 0-918471-67-2
    1. Roy, Lindy—Exhibitions. 2. Architecture—United States—20th
century—Exhibitions. I. Roy, Lindy. II. San Francisco Museum
of Modern Art. III. Title. IV. Series.
NA737.R684 2003
720'.92—dc21
                        2002154628

contents

Poolhouse, Sagaponac, New York,
2000–, nighttime view

director's foreword

NEAL BENEZRA

Dedicated to the architect Lindy Roy, this is the first in a series of exhibitions and publications conceived by Joseph Rosa, the Museum's Helen Hilton Raiser Curator of Architecture and Design. With the goal of showcasing the work of architects, graphic designers, and industrial designers who are revitalizing their respective disciplines, the Design Series is a natural extension of SFMOMA's design-related activities. Since its establishment two decades ago, the Architecture and Design Department has been at the forefront of tracking trends and innovations in the field. Today, as a new generation of practitioners is changing the way our built environment is conceptualized and theorized, the series will enable the Museum to measure the state of design more accurately as well as more critically.

As an architect who is just coming to international prominence, Lindy Roy is an ideal subject for the series' inaugural volume. Although only a few of her designs have been realized to date, she has emerged as one of the most outstanding and provocative figures on the contemporary scene. As Joseph Rosa points out in his insightful essay, her sensitive responses to problems of site, technology, economy, and construction have resulted in a number of ground-breaking projects that have much to suggest about where the discipline is heading. Published at a moment when several of her designs are reaching fruition, this catalogue represents an important document of Roy's most significant projects as well as an exploration of what happens when methods once considered solely experimental or conceptual are applied to architecture that is not just buildable but eminently practical.

Joseph Rosa joins me in thanking Lindy Roy for opening her studio and life to everyone involved in the production of this exhibition and its related publication. Heidi Werner and her colleagues at ROY provided helpful access to information and images. We are indebted to Elaine McKeon, the Board of Trustees, and Helen Hilton Raiser for their tireless advocacy of the Museum's architecture and design programming as well as the Architecture and Design Forum and Accessions committees for their work on the department's behalf. Ruth Berson, deputy director, programs and collections, was a helpful supporter of this project from its earliest stages, as were curators Janet Bishop, Madeleine Grynsztejn, Douglas R. Nickel, Sandra S. Phillips, John Weber, and Benjamin Weil. Curatorial associate Darrin Alfred played an essential role in the shaping of this project, providing the catalogue's informative project descriptions and sharing ideas throughout the development of the exhibition. A number of other staff members contributed time and expertise to this project, including Michelle Barger, associate conservator; Alexander Cheves, museum preparator; Chad Coerver, acting director of publications; Steve Dye, exhibitions technical manager; Karen A. Levine, editor; Terril Neely, senior designer; Jessica O'Dwyer, public relations associate; Kent Roberts, exhibitions design manager; Thomas Shannon, chief preparator; Jennifer Siekert, exhibitions coordinator; Cassandra Smith, assistant registrar; Jill Sterrett, director of collections and conservation; Peter Stevenson, manager of public programs; Lia Tjandra, designer; and Greg Wilson, senior preparator. Thanks also go to curatorial associate Ruth Keffer and administrative assistant Amy Ress for their invaluable assistance with all Architecture and Design Department activities.

Okavango Delta Spa, Botswana,
1997–, view of guest unit

algorithmic foldings:
the architecture of lindy roy

JOSEPH ROSA

Throughout the history of modern architecture, there are rare moments when the strength and vision of a single design can establish a career. From Giovanni Battista Piranesi's haunting eighteenth-century renderings of cavernous imaginary spaces called *The Prisons* to Zaha Hadid's winning 1982 entry for the Peak Project in Hong Kong, architects have continually sought to dissolve the boundaries between the reality of architecture and what it could be. Lindy Roy's 1997 proposal for the Okavango Delta Spa in Botswana is one of those rare designs that fit into this trajectory. In many ways it established her as a leading voice in the new generation of digitally literate architects now exploring uncharted aesthetic territory. With a marked ecological sensitivity, Roy's design ideology incorporates disparate spheres ranging from natural science to technology, creating algorithmic systems to generate an architecture that is simultaneously respectful of context and program, experimental in resolution, and, above all, feasible.

Roy is in many ways an anomaly in the genealogy of contemporary architecture. She takes a very modern, almost nomadic approach to her work, and she is also one of the few female architects who do not have a male business partner. Based in New York, her studio, ROY, is not rooted in a mid-century modern revisionist sensibility, but rather a forward-thinking, futuristic optimism that, aesthetically, could also be called essentialist. Her design methodology reduces projects to their fundamental characteristics and then reconstructs them through a contextual and experientially derived prism. Digital technology also plays a significant role in Roy's studio, from the creation of early conceptual frameworks to the final fabrication of architectural components.

Roy attributes her nomadic tendency to "the immigrant desire to see and learn everything." Born in Cape Town, South Africa, in 1963, Roy received a bachelor's degree in architecture from the University of Cape Town in 1985. Unable to reconcile the tensions of life under apartheid and eager to experience other cultures, Roy moved to New York shortly after finishing her studies. In 1988 she returned to school and received a master's in architecture in 1990 from Columbia University's Graduate School of Architecture, Planning, and Preservation, under the new direction of Bernard Tschumi. Remaining true to her credo, "If things are not happening for you, then move to where they can happen," by the end of 1993 Roy had already traversed the country once to work for Franklin D. Israel in Los Angeles before returning to Manhattan to spend two years with Peter D. Eisenman. In 1994 she left for New Orleans to teach at Tulane University's School of Architecture, and a year later she moved to Houston for two years for a position at Rice University's School of Architecture. In the fall of 1998 Roy returned to New York to establish her practice; since then she has been teaching at the Cooper Union, Princeton University, and Columbia University architecture programs.[1] In the relatively short period of time since the commission for the spa in 1997, Roy's solutions for affordable and luxury houses, commercial spaces, and eco-resorts have showcased her ability as an analytical thinker capable of mediating the academic and buildable worlds of architecture.

The ideologies of promising designers such as Lindy Roy must be seen in the context of a radical shift that took place in the teaching and practice of architecture in the seventies. Prior to then, young graduates would typically go into the profession, establish a career through building, and then return to the academy to teach. However, the economic decline of the late seventies resulted in fewer job opportunities for young designers, leading many to enter academia without ever having practiced. This generation questioned normative architectural education and pushed its boundaries to be more inclusive of ancillary disciplines and their methods of critique. The postwar International Style, based on functionalism and standardization, was soon rejected by critically minded younger architects who equated this corporate style with the banality of modern culture. Combined with a renewed interest in handcrafted objects, their embrace of methodologies from other disciplines—including the semiotics, post-structuralism, and deconstruction of literary and film theory—succeeded in generating a novel critical framework for contemporary architecture.

By the late eighties the economy began to show promise, and limited competitions for new buildings reflected the ideals that were circulating among architects who were finally getting a chance to build. A hitherto unseen breed of academics began attempting to bridge the gap between the theories of architecture taught in the classroom and their practical application. The 1988 *Deconstructivist Architecture* exhibition at New York's Museum of Modern Art, organized by Philip Johnson and Mark Wigley, helped to solidify this period of architectural invention in a codifiable package, in the process canonizing the work of designers Peter Eisenman, Bernard Tschumi, Zaha Hadid, Frank Gehry, Daniel Libeskind, Rem Koolhaas, and the office of CoopHimmelblau. Although competition jurors singled out promising schemes such as Hadid's Peak Project for Hong Kong and Libeskind's Jewish Museum for Berlin, by the end of the eighties only a few buildings had actually been built to reflect these new ideologies: Eisenman's Wexner Center for the Arts in Columbus, Ohio; Gehry's additions to his home in Santa Monica, California; Tschumi's Parc de La Villette in Paris; John Hedjuk's apartment building in Berlin; and a few additions to Los Angeles houses by Tom Mayne and Michael Rotondi of Morphosis and Eric Owen Moss.

Not surprisingly, the individuals who designed these works and their colleagues in the *Deconstructivist Architecture* exhibition held appointments as deans, chairs, and professors in university architecture programs. By the late eighties and early nineties, these architects and their affiliated institutions had become synonymous with avant-garde methodologies, and some of the best new critical approaches in architectural design were being explored and debated at the academic level. These developments were also due in part to the introduction of digital design and production methods in the studio. Students (as well as instructors) could now rethink past methods of conceptualization and construction to generate forms characterized as smooth, supple, and morphed.[2]

The younger set that changed the academy in the late seventies completely retooled architectural pedagogy, producing students who are more aesthetically informed and understand critical theory, digital design, and building technologies. The latest generation of digitally literate designers has taken the academy's earlier level of architectural discourse and fused it into practices that are emblematic of designers like Roy, Greg Lynn, and SHoP, just to name a few.

The commission for the Okavango Delta Spa (1997–; pp. 16–19) came to Lindy Roy while she was teaching at Rice University in Houston. The concept behind the spa was to merge the world of the sophisticated traveler with the bush experience. The site is truly a rare setting; not only is it the only delta in the world that ends in a desert, but it is also quite remote, accessible only by helicopter or bush plane. The environmentally sensitive landscape requires minimal intervention, making it essential that the freestanding pavilions or "pods" that comprise the spa be tethered and floating rather than set into the ground with foundation walls. The floating pods also address the condition that the owners, old friends of Roy's from South Africa, will be responsible for removing everything from the site if the business fails.[3]

Roy employed a two-pronged strategy regarding local resources for building the spa, a tactic that reappears in many of her later commissions. Inspired by indigenous construction techniques, she reconfigured the region's vernacular thatched roofs with steeper slopes to allow for better drainage, and she then adjusted them to prevailing wind patterns, resulting in an overall shape that is hyperbolic and sculptural in form. She also acknowledged local crafts by weaving translucent fiber-optic strands—similar in diameter to the reeds and straw traditionally used in Botswana—into guardrails along the spa's walkways. Roy's use of fiber optics represents a harnessing of new technologies for tactile effect as well as an abiding interest in fusing different cultural systems of construction. (The idea is developed further in Roy's designs for the Issey Miyake store and Noah bar, both in Manhattan.)

It is helpful to think of Roy's approach to architecture as algorithmic. This is not to say that her process derives from mathematical equations, but rather that it involves a deliberate series of responses to architectural problems, drawing on a range of information to generate a cohesive aesthetic solution. This methodology and its implementation are best reflected in the spa's overall master plan. Below water level, an infrastructure of pumps, pipes, and supports creates a matrix that allows the site to function in extreme conditions. Above water level is a more topographical composition of elements, such as the curvilinear walkways that are tethered to abandoned termite mounds and lead to individual pods. Viewed as an algorithmic system of parts, the spa becomes a conceptual "readymade," a work of nomadic architecture that can be resituated anywhere in the delta.

The pods collectively evoke a provisional setting. Set in a natural papyrus clearing, each unit's enclosure comprises a low deck with a massage table and chair, a slightly raised area for sleeping, and a tethered fiberglass bathroom unit. The pods' adjustable outer skin is a structured, transparent, high-strength tent fabric that follows the perimeter of the roof from which it is suspended. Inside this form is a looser layer of mosquito netting. The propeller-like roof planes project beyond the pod enclosures; when the operable tent surface is deployed, it encloses the fiberglass bathroom unit along with a small area of the delta for total privacy. However, the most exhilarating of Roy's design resolutions embodies the ultimate juxtaposition of the bush experience and spa opulence in the form of a motorized lap pool. The steel section of the pool is fabricated in a gauge that can resist the force of crocodile jaws. A thin wire mesh of steel is fastened inside the pool area, allowing guests to swim in the filtered delta, and the perimeter of the pool is wrapped in a wooden deck that incorporates chaises.

Roy's ability to take a preexisting condition and heighten it to produce a viable model for eco-tourism is indicative of her ability to generate architecture that has presence yet is provisional to its context. This can also be seen in her later projects, many of which expand on research for the Okavango Delta Spa. The VHouse (1999–; pp. 20–23), for example, designed for the Fifth Ward in Houston, is an alternative to poorly designed affordable housing for low-income families. Having lived in Houston from 1995 to 1998, Roy understood the urban fabric of the city and its humid climate. Her plan modifies the typology of the shotgun house to create a residence designed around prevailing winds, thus reducing the inhabitants' dependence on air-conditioning. Since the postwar period, the advent of air-conditioning has made year-round destinations out of many American cities formerly considered only seasonally habitable. While this is fine for resort towns such as Palm Springs, California, the situation has been quite the opposite for communities such as the Fifth Ward, where the cost of air-conditioning is prohibitive. Homes designed to rely on air-conditioning tend not to have floor plans that allow for easy cross-ventilation. Surprisingly, however, the simple layout of the shotgun shack provides an enfilade of rooms that permits the building to take advantage of natural air flow.

To make the shotgun typology work with the site, Roy created an algorithmic framework of information based on data about the area's wind patterns. Her research led her to lift the roof plane, twisting and extending the front toward the breeze, which is drawn through the house by a series of ceiling fans. The extruded roof, which folds and bends over the house's simple rectilinear footprint, cantilevers over a large front porch that visually extends the open-plan configuration of the living room, dining room, and kitchen. Another important element of the design makes use of adjacent street lighting. Roy sets the highest point of the roof ridge at the same height as the exterior streetlight, borrowing light to illuminate the underside of the porch's ceiling and providing an inviting exterior space where families can gather, have a visible presence, and play an active role in reclaiming their community.

Shortly after the VHouse competition, Roy was invited to design a residence in Sagaponac, New York, where the developer Harry ("Coco") Brown Jr. has asked thirty-six international architects to create weekend homes in the modern idiom.[4] The Poolhouse (2000–; pp. 26–29) might at first seem like a departure from Roy's explorations in algorithmic systems. It is a very contextual design, specific to the evolution of the weekend homes that have populated the area since the fifties, but it also serves as a critique of the culture that inspired it. Roy's design is reminiscent of classic Long Island summer homes by Charles

Gwathmey, Richard Meier, and Barbara and Julian Neski (below), but she has transformed typical elements of the genre to reveal the pleasure culture's inherent qualities of spectacle and voyeurism.[5] The simple two-story home has an open plan with the living room, dining room, and kitchen on the first floor and three bedrooms with adjacent balconies upstairs. A three-story "water wall" (comprising bathrooms, steam room, wet bar, and lap pool) bifurcates the rectangular shape of the house, visually anchoring it in the landscape. In the traditional weekend home plan, the pool is placed adjacent to the house, bordered by a deck, and displayed through a series of large glass doors that open the house to its surroundings. With her monolithic water wall, however, Roy literally blurs boundaries between indoors and out, making the pool an event space inside as well as outside the house.

Barbara and Julian Neski,
Bridgehampton House, Long
Island, New York, 1970

Roy's pursuit of clarity and definition brings the structural vocabulary of the weekend home into play. Most modern examples were inexpensively built with simple wood-frame or post-in-beam construction, while the more opulent homes featured steel-frame construction (providing for larger uninterrupted expanses of glass). Roy deploys the concept of clear spans in a sequence of S-shaped steel frames that incorporate the floor, column, and roofing members. Clad in stainless steel, these simple forms create double cantilevers that bend once at the second floor and again at the roof. The structural two-story steel extrusion allows flexibility in the overall design of the house while accommodating the programmed volumes. An adjustable wood slat-wrap skin sinuously envelops the exterior of the Poolhouse; this seemingly continuous surface is employed horizontally on roofs, decks, and exterior walls and modulates light levels in the home. A concrete slab at the first floor gently bends and folds over the steel structure, creating a series of interior and exterior elements that include the exterior wall of the kitchen and a bench in the dining room. This fluid gesture recalls the folded roof plane of the VHouse, where a straightforward movement effects a change in function and program. The formal device of bending and folding appears intermittently throughout Roy's designs, from small-scale interior surfaces to larger exterior forms.

Roy's Cancer Alley project (2001–; pp. 36–37), a collaboration with the photographer Richard Misrach, inverts the cultural typology of barges on the Mississippi River to generate a new environmental infrastructure for ailing communities in Louisiana. For Roy, this particular design is more data- and research-driven and less about a formal aesthetic resolution. Cancer Alley is an eighty-mile stretch along the Mississippi between Baton Rouge and New Orleans. With some 150 petrochemical plants, the region is reported to have one of the country's most dangerous concentrations of toxic emissions, and its low-income residents have very high rates of cancer, asthma, and other medical ailments. After photographing in the area, Misrach asked Roy to design an intervention for a linear site. She proposed programming the ubiquitous industrial barges that travel the river with educational, recreational, and leisure facilities. Dedicated to different purposes, such as hotels, drive-in theaters, sports facilities, or vegetable gardens (below), the barges—like commuter trains—would work on a timetable, moving from town to town. For Roy, the project is a way to reclaim contaminated land, retooling the countryside into a fluid "convertible space" where program and need can adapt hourly. Cancer Alley illustrates Roy's ability to think algorithmically by folding abstract concepts, regional history, and innovation into a coherent resolution that speaks to aesthetics, typology, and cultural ideology.

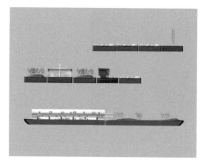

Cancer Alley, Mississippi River, Louisiana, 2001–, view of swimming pool and elevation of barge configuration. Photographic material courtesy of Richard Misrach

The idea of merging "convertible space," fiber optics, off-the-shelf hardware, and multifunctional cultural interpretations can best be seen in Roy's design for Noah (2001–; pp. 30–33), a bar in Manhattan. Located in a defunct meatpacking facility, the existing space is left largely unaltered. Above the heavy-duty tracks that once carried meat is a weave of optical fiber that traverses the length of the space and spells out the name of the bar at the entrance. Roy has reconfigured the system for moving meat as a rack for hanging resin tables and red leather chaises. Notwithstanding the double entendre associated with the bar and its original function, Roy has created a truly modern space by infusing an existing structure with a new program that is, in a strange way, contextual.

In the summer of 2001 Roy was selected from a shortlist of competitors by the jurors of the MoMA/P.S.1 Young Architects Program to design a summer installation for P.S.1 Contemporary Art Center in Long Island City, New York. Roy's design, titled *subWave* (pp. 34–35), transformed P.S.1's courtyard into a spa-like setting. Twelve steel-framed pivoting hammocks rotated on wheels, surrounded by ultraviolet-screening canopies. Oscillating fans attached to a long concrete wall produced a continual breeze over three pools of water. Employing wind, spray, water, and shade—elements that have been part of her vocabulary since the Okavango Delta Spa—Roy created an urban oasis with a unique microclimate. The project's three-month gestation from conception to construction proved that Roy could produce in a very short period of time. More importantly, this temporary installation was her first realized commission. *SubWave* received critical acclaim and led to Roy's first major commercial commission, the new Manhattan showroom for the furniture manufacturer Vitra.[6]

In both intention and execution, Roy's design for Vitra (2001–2002; pp. 38–41), with its large folding surfaces that unite the different levels, represents an evolution of the architect's algorithmic process. Impressed by the "ingenious spatial solutions" of her earlier projects, Vitra asked Roy to convert space in a turn-of-the-century Meatpacking District warehouse.[7] Disposed over three adjacent stories, the 13,000-square-foot store contains a street-level retail floor, a lower-level gallery, and a second floor for offices and a showroom. To mediate these isolated industrial spaces, Roy removed portions of the existing slabs of the first and second floors to link them together visually and allow stair circulation. A large, seemingly continuous rubber "tongue" folds and bends vertically and horizontally through openings in the floor, offering visual clues to spaces above and below. While this surface appears to be suspended or floating above the floor planes, it also functions as a support for the display of Vitra's furniture line.

Roy's Wind River Lodge (2001–; pp. 42–45), an extreme skiing facility in southern Alaska, employs the fold to create a complete, sinuous structure. Here the building's surface conceptually bends back onto itself at either end to create a twenty-six-room hotel—whose sloping form is reminiscent of a ski jump—and a shape called "the ski helmet" that houses a control tower and bar with panoramic views of the peaks beyond. Traversing this sculptural form is a simple rectangle that accommodates three helipads and bridges the two buildings. The heliport is essential to the heliski experience, in which people are transported by helicopter to otherwise inaccessible glacial peaks, and the lodge is intended for a select audience of adrenaline seekers. As with Roy's earlier explorations in deploying folded forms in contextual settings, here the curved outlines of the building sit lightly on the site. The hotel's overall structure rests on large pier walls that are perpendicular to the sculptural cross section of the building, and the helmet form is supported by columns, freeing the ground plane underneath. Between the two buildings, the helipad platform stretches into the landscape, placed atop an enclosed glass warehouse for equipment storage.

The monolithic shape of Wind River Lodge is composed of galvanized steel extrusions, produced with the aid of digital technology to ensure precision and fabricated in transportable sizes that can be barged and trucked to the site for assembly.[8] Insulated curtain walls with floor-to-ceiling glass enclose either side of the hotel, where large industrial metal louvers are used horizontally to modulate the quality of light. (In summer the site receives up to twenty hours of daylight, which gradually transforms the snow-covered landscape into a lush, green riverside retreat that is accessible by road.)

As Roy has moved on to design larger structures, her strategy of bending and folding forms and her approach to overall massing have created metanarratives of each project's program, inspired by the nature of the actual sites. In the winter, for example, Wind River Lodge is integrated with its environment, while in the summer it becomes a characterization of the winter landscape. Something similar occurs in her scheme

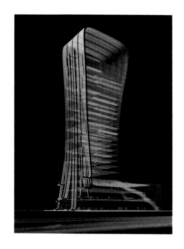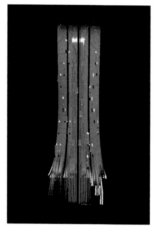

West Street Tower, New York, 2002,
street perspective and side elevation

for a twenty-eight-story housing unit on the Lower West Side of Manhattan, where the highway conceptually wraps the building on its north/south axis. In response to the polarizing official proposals for the former site of the World Trade Center, the *New York Times'* architecture critic, Herbert Muschamp, organized an alternate master plan for reimagining downtown New York (each team invited to participate was asked to design a speculative building).[9] Assigned a spot above a section of the West Street highway, which Muschamp's team suggests should be run underground as a tunnel, Roy designed an upscale building (above) that uses the site as a metaphor for its structure. The sides of the apartment block extrude at the base, making it appear as if the highway were literally moving over the glass-clad building.

The formal evolution of Roy's work in recent years reveals a marked talent for turning architectural ideology into buildable reality. Her capacity to think of architecture algorithmically—a strategy that results in innovative answers to problems of culture, site, program, and context—has generated a body of work that might be termed essentialist in aesthetic. Whether on the scale of a temporary installation or an urban or weekend residence, her designs unite gestures of provisional intervention with an imposing sense of presence, yielding lyrical buildings that interrogate traditional notions of location, use, and typology. Roy's characteristic ribbonlike surfaces, which fold gently into the structure or the landscape, point the way for a new generation of twenty-first-century architects.

NOTES

1. Lindy Roy, interview by author, 19 August 2002.   2. For more on digital design in architecture, see my publication *Folds, Blobs, and Boxes: Architecture in the Digital Era* (Pittsburgh: Heinz Architectural Center, Carnegie Museum of Art, 2001). Also see Alicia Imperiale, *New Flatness: Surface Tension in Digital Architecture* (Basel: Birkaüser, 2000); Ned Cramer and Anne Guiney, "The Computer School," *Architecture* (September 2000): 94–107; and Annette Le Cuyer, "Designs on the Computer," *Architectural Review* (January 1995): 76–79.   3. Roy, interview by author, 15 August 2002.   4. Carole Paquette, "One Subdivision, Thirty-Six Architects with a Modernist Flair," *New York Times* (22 September 2002).   5. For more on classic modern weekend houses in the Hamptons, see Alastair Gordon, *Weekend Utopia* (New York: Princeton Architectural Press, 1999). Also see Paul Goldberger, *Houses of the Hamptons* (New York: Alfred A. Knopf, 1986) and the work of Charles Gwathmey and Richard Meier in *Five Architects* (New York: Wittenborn and Company, 1972).   6. Roy, interview by author, 28 August 2002. 7. Jen Renzi, "Extreme Measures," *Interior Design* (November 2001): 140.   8. Roy, interview by author, 2 September 2002. A similar method of construction was recently employed by Foreign Office Architecture in building the Yokohama International Port Terminal in Japan.   9. Herbert Muschamp, "Thinking Big: A Plan for Ground Zero and Beyond," *New York Times Magazine* (8 September 2002).

projects

okavango delta spa
okavango river delta, botswana
1997–

Designed for the private safari company Uncharted
Africa, the Okavango Delta Spa will be constructed deep within northern Botswana's Okavango
River Delta, a dynamic stretch of water covering more than nine thousand square miles of the
otherwise arid Kalahari Desert. Accessible only by small airplane or helicopter, this two-acre
holistic health retreat comprises "a series of fixed, tethered, and free elements," introducing the
comforts of a resort to an extreme natural environment.

Seven open-air, wood-framed, thatch-roofed guest accommodations are individually placed
within natural clearings of the site's six- to eight-foot-high papyrus beds. These plantlike "pods,"
which appear to float like petals on the water's surface, are actually secured to the delta floor.
The pods' canopies spiral into the wetlands, offering protection from the elements while allowing
guests to "indulge in the natural environment." Responding to changing seasonal water levels,
a small floating fiberglass unit containing a bathroom is moored to each lodging. The guest
pods are connected in pairs by a network of buoyant fiberglass-and-wood walkways that are
anchored to and wrapped around islands formed from the remains of abandoned termite
mounds. Solar-powered fiber-optic cables are woven into the guardrails, lighting the walkways

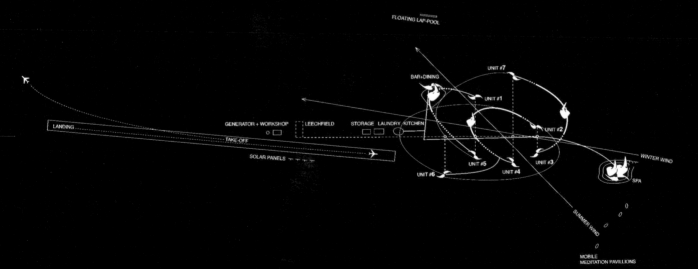

FLOATING LAP-POOL

UNIT #7

BAR+DINING

UNIT #1

LANDING

GENERATOR + WORKSHOP   LEECHFIELD   STORAGE LAUNDRY KITCHEN

UNIT #2

TAKE-OFF

WINTER WIND

SOLAR PANELS

UNIT #5   UNIT #4   UNIT #3

UNIT #6

SPA

SUMMER WIND

MOBILE
MEDITATION PAVILLIONS

N

From top: mobile lap pool;
conceptual site section

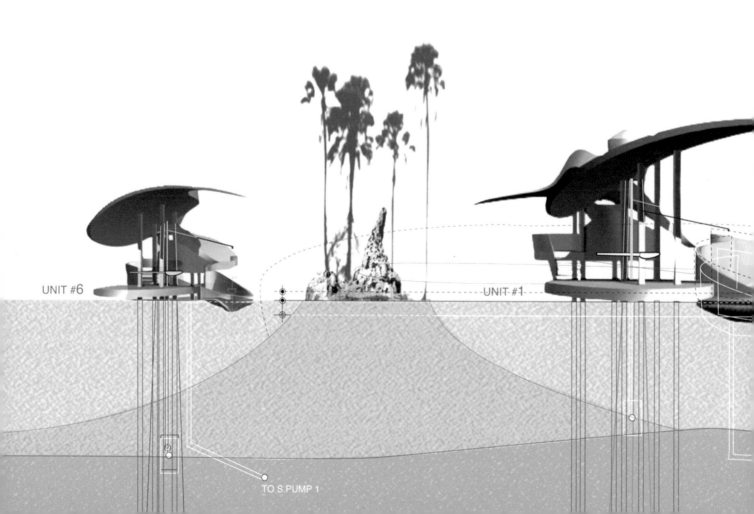

UNIT #6

UNIT #1

TO S.PUMP 1

by night. Two larger structures house the health spa center, bar, and dining pavilion. The project's most unique features are its free elements—mobile meditation spaces and a crocodile-resistant lap pool—which are powered with outboard motors so they can be maneuvered through the delta's inlets.

Responding to its peculiar context, the spa's aesthetic is characterized by the playful use of opposing elements, drawing on and giving architectural form to the contrasts and rhythms of the Okavango Delta. Free to traverse the site, the resort's assorted structures provide a heightened awareness of the friction between nature and culture. In seeking to communicate this juxtaposition, Roy exploits the delta landscape as an integral part of the design, a place of common ground where the natural and constructed meet.

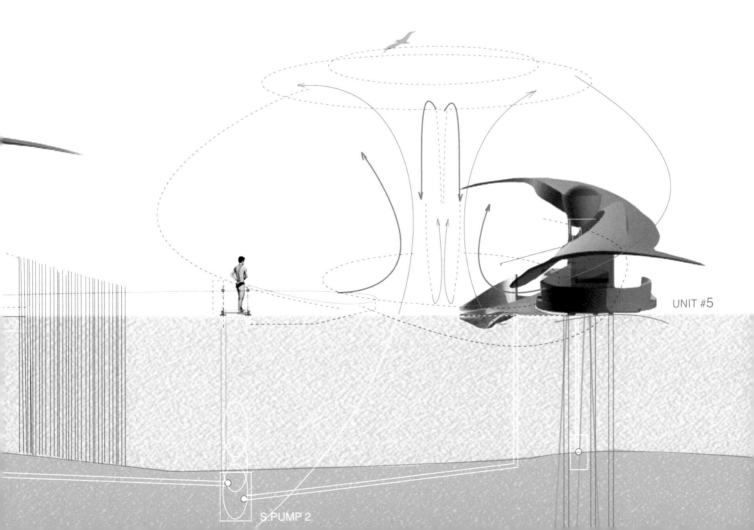

UNIT #5

S.PUMP 2

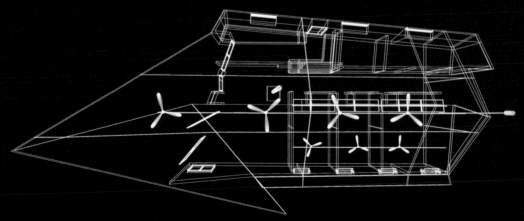

vhouse
houston
1999–

Commissioned in 1999 for *Sixteen Houses: Owning a House in the City,* an exhibition at Houston's DiverseWorks gallery, the VHouse is an innovative prototype for affordable single-family homes. Working in collaboration with the nonprofit Fifth Ward Community Redevelopment Corporation, the architect Michael Bell asked sixteen design teams to propose inexpensive residences for a once-thriving, historically rich black neighborhood in Houston. With results ranging from highly conceptual to quietly traditional, six of the projects, including Roy's, were selected by jury to be constructed under a new federal voucher program providing down-payment assistance to low-income families.

Roy's 1,450-square-foot, three-bedroom house is a contemporary variation on traditional shotgun-style homes—long, narrow, single-story residences whose affordability made them accessible to generations of low-income families. With cost-effective wood framing clad in galvanized sheet metal, glass, and Viroc (cement-bonded particleboard that is smooth in texture and light gray in color), the durable, flexible, and economical design addresses typical urban issues, particularly the house's relationship to its surroundings. Running perpendicular to the street, the folding, pitched metal roof twists up toward the streetlights, serving almost, according to Bell, "as a lampshade." The raised porch below provides a sheltered spot to sit and chat with neighbors on a hot summer afternoon. Above the porch, a ceiling fan hangs from a suspended scaffold of metal piping that pierces the house lengthwise, supporting a series of fans on the interior and ending outside the back door with a bug zapper.

As in traditional shotgun homes, the interior space is defined by a single hallway that leads directly from front to back door. However, Roy has placed the communal areas of the house—living room, dining room, and kitchen—within an open, double-height space near the front of the plan. This contemporary update further opens and extends the home's dialogue with its urban environment. The private spaces—three bedrooms and two baths—are appropriately tucked along the corridor toward the rear of the house.

21

From top: front elevation;
rear elevation; plan view
Opposite page: street perspective

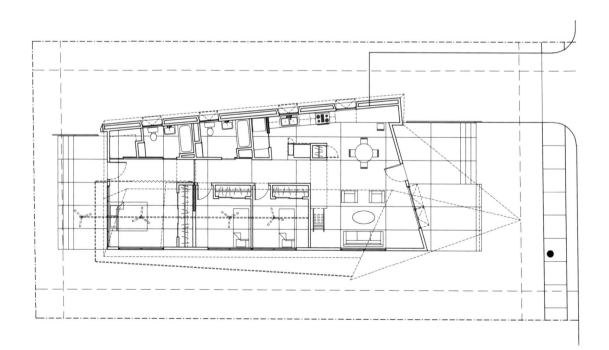

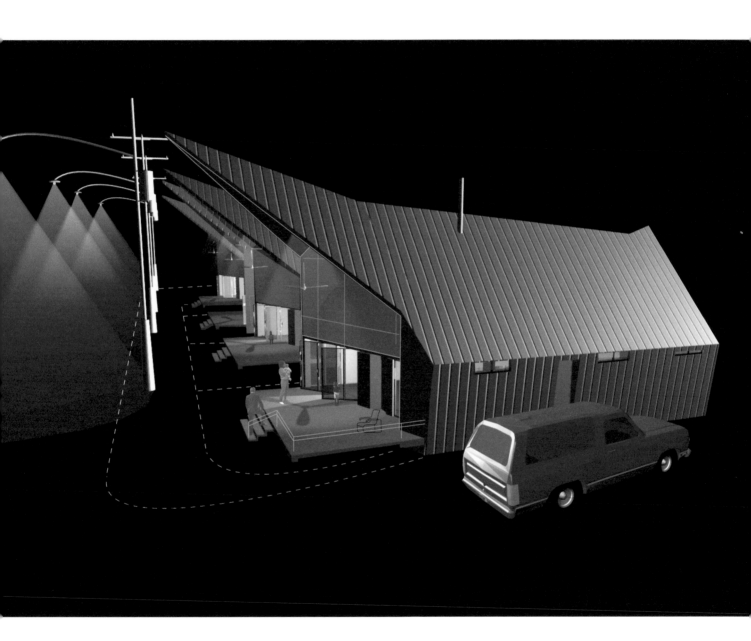

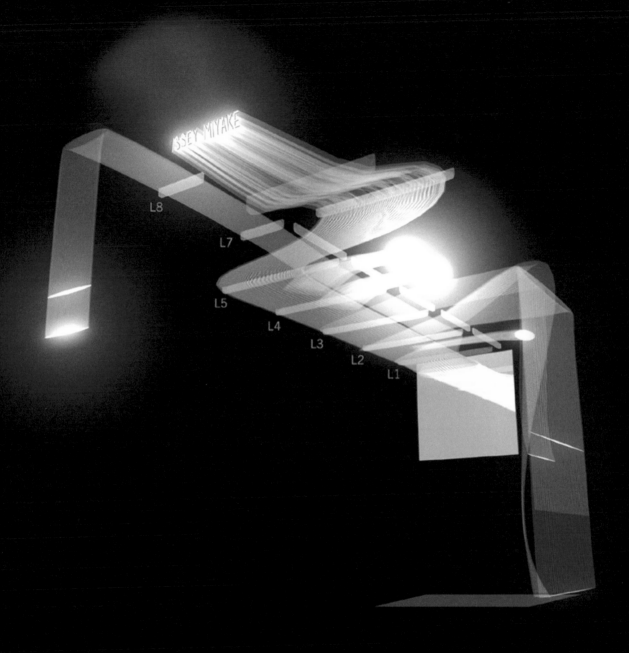

ISSEY MIYAKE

L8

L7

L5

L4

L3

L2

L1

Side view of fiber-optic lighting
Opposite page: conceptual section

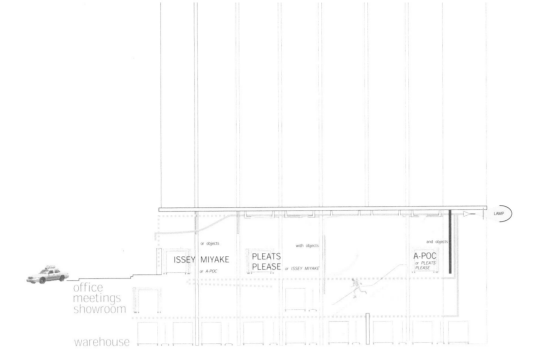

or objects

with objects

and objects

ISSEY MIYAKE
or A-POC

PLEATS
PLEASE *or ISSEY MIYAKE*

A-POC
or PLEATS PLEASE

LAMP

office
meetings
showroom

warehouse

issey miyake
new york
2000

Conceived as the new U.S. headquarters for the fashion house Issey Miyake, this 9,000-square-foot space was designed for a landmark cast-iron building in New York's Tribeca neighborhood. Drawn up for an invitational competition, the proposal provides a place for all of Miyake's commercial clothing lines to be shown alongside previously unavailable collections. Incorporating three floors, a fiber-optic system is distributed throughout the location, effectively linking the first-floor showroom with offices and meeting rooms in the basement and a warehouse in the subbasement.

Inspired by the neural networks of the human brain, a densely interconnected structure of continuous fiber-optic strands emerges from a "light engine" concealed behind a large mirrored wall at the rear of the first floor. Emulating the visual properties of textiles and other woven materials, bundles of the flexible strands are suspended from existing wooden beams. While some fibers glow along their length, others emit light where they are cut. The variable light field comes alive as it pulsates above the showroom floor and energizes the room, both engaging and provoking the shopper.

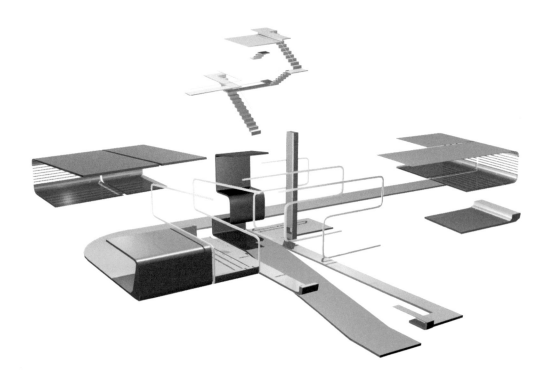

poolhouse
sagaponac, new york
2000–

The Poolhouse was designed for a heavily wooded residential area on Long Island, New York. Known as the Houses at Sagaponac, the community is a major planned initiative by the developer Harry ("Coco") Brown Jr., who has invited more than thirty international architects to create informal, unpretentious homes that are intimately related to nature as well as ecologically and economically responsible.

The volume of the 3,400-square-foot summer house is defined by a succession of eight S-shaped steel frames that support protective layers of wood and glass. These folded planes—which allow floor, wall, and ceiling to flow as one—combine compositionally to provide a ground floor characterized by graceful rectangular spaces for the kitchen, dining, and living areas. Lined by an expanse of pivoting glass doors, the perimeter of the ground floor opens out to the garden beyond. Louvered wood cladding follows the curving profile of the upper story. Wrapping the exterior of the residence, the louvers afford flexible levels of privacy to the three bedrooms and two adjacent terraces at the top of the house while allowing for a modifiable range of light on the interior. The swimming pool—the experience around which the house was designed—further blurs the distinctions between inside and out as it reaches into the house and passes through the

Perspective view
Opposite page: exploded axonometric diagram

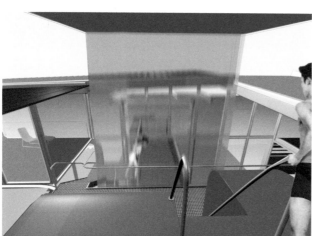

From top: approach from driveway; interior
view from carport; view from pool; water wall
Opposite page, from top: section; plans
of first floor (left) and second floor (right)

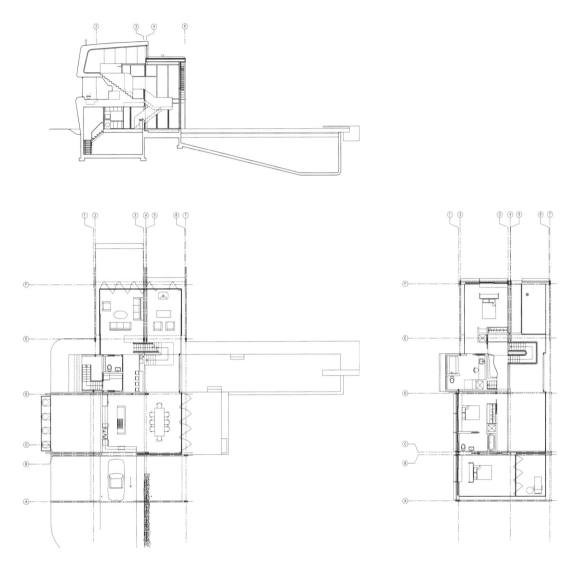

living room, integrating all liquid elements (lap pool, steam room, wet bar, and bathrooms) in a three-story blue mosaic-tiled "water wall." A series of concrete slabs flow between interior and exterior as they travel over the stainless steel-clad S-frames. The concrete driveway bends up as it approaches the house, forming the exterior wall of the kitchen, entry, and dining room seating. The living room floor extends to become an outdoor terrace with fireside seating.

According to Roy, the Poolhouse's simple, elegant, and modest concept "embraces the informality and pleasure of the summer house." Interior and exterior spaces provide a sense of structure while mingling with the surrounding landscape, effectively capturing the spirit of mid-twentieth-century weekend homes in the Hamptons and the steel-and-glass houses of Southern California.

Conceptual studies
Opposite page: view of bar interior

noah
new york
2001–

No longer defined solely by the industry for which it was named, Manhattan's Meatpacking District is undergoing rapid gentrification. Tucked away in what was once a refrigerated meat locker, this 2,200-square-foot bar acknowledges the neighborhood's past while serving witness to the dramatic changes affecting its streets and warehouses, where animal carcasses continue to be butchered and processed next door to newly opened upscale restaurants, galleries, nightclubs, and boutiques. Adding high-tech fiber optics to the site's existing structure, Roy's design "seeks to utilize the meatpacking infrastructure and to redefine it according to a new program: a bar."

An extensive system of ceiling-mounted steel tracks, once used to unload carcasses from trucks into coolers, now supports a collection of custom-made furniture. Suspended on threaded rods, blood-red leather chaises and translucent cast-resin tables are free to move within the field of tracks and switches. Adjustable to heights suitable for standing, sitting, or lounging, this adaptive structure allows the reconfiguration of the space for almost any need.

Like Roy's project for Issey Miyake, Noah exploits the effects of fiber-optic lighting. Three optical fiber bundles pass through openings in the existing concrete floor. Powered by a basement light engine, the fibers form a curtain at the street facade. Each bundle splits into three "light braids" that climb the steel scaffold in a plaited weave, forming an organic "light field." As two bundles travel toward the rear to screen off a section of the bar and the bathrooms, the third loops back toward the street to write the storefront sign with the cut ends of its fibers. The lighting system inside the bar mimics a fiber-optic grid recently installed throughout the Meatpacking District by the local phone company. The laying of fiber-optic cable for the neighborhood's new technophiles is just one way that the city of New York is recognizing the district's evolving identity.

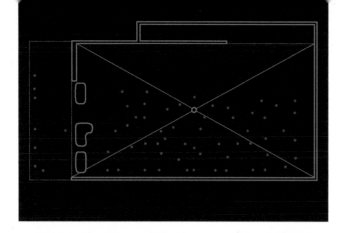

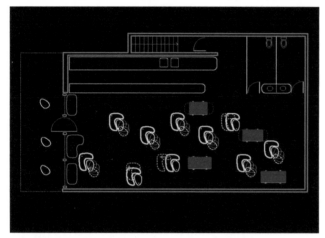

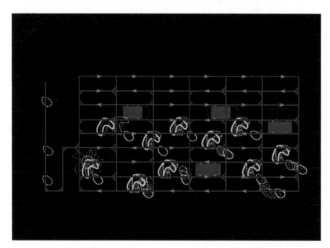

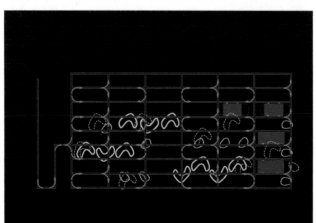

Plan diagrams showing possible furniture configurations
Opposite page, from top: detail of fiber-optic lighting
system; detail of interior elevation with fiber optics
and furniture

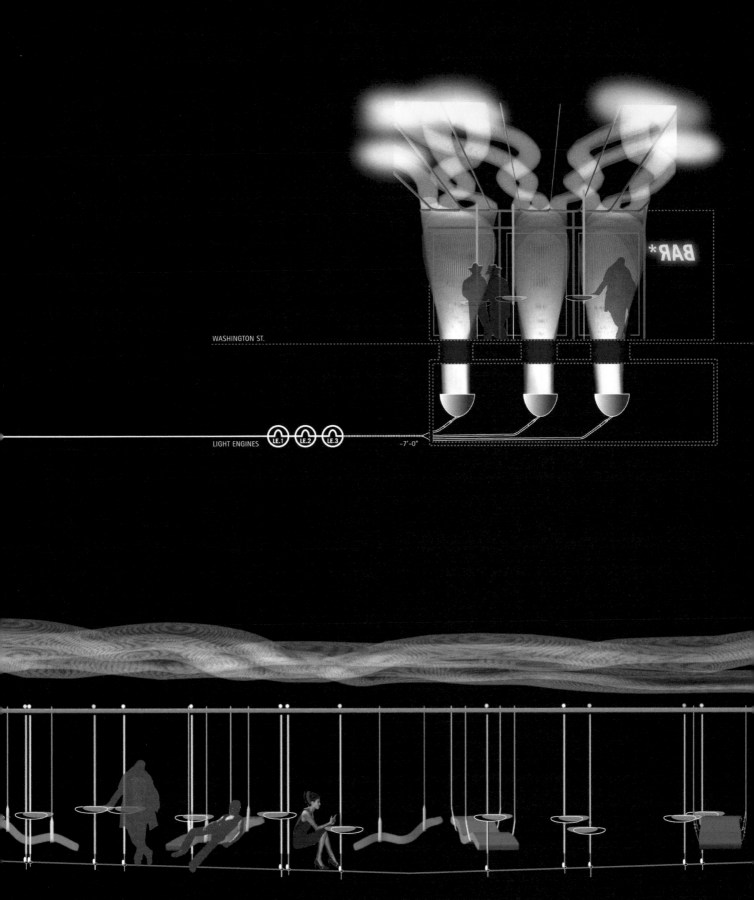

WASHINGTON ST.

LIGHT ENGINES   L.E.1 L.E.2 L.E.3   -7'-0"

BAR*

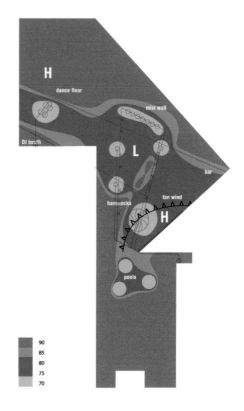

	90
	85
	80
	75
	70

subwave
long island city, new york
2001

Roy was selected from a group of five finalists as the winner of the 2001 MoMA/P.S.1 Young Architects Program, an annual competition that gives emerging architects an opportunity to build projects at P.S.1's Queens facility. Sited in the converted school's courtyard, the resulting installation, titled *subWave,* featured a layered infrastructure of climate modifiers that distributed wind, water, and shade. On view during the summer of 2001, the multiuse environment functioned as both an "urban oasis" from the heat and as host to the contemporary art center's *Warm Up* series, a festival offering an eclectic mix of architecture and music.

Divided into three parts—climate, activity, and supplies—Roy's design transformed the concrete and gravel space into a dystopic, futuristic setting inspired, in part, by the New York subway and the science-fiction movie *Coma.* Hanging from a rudimentary steel structure, canvas, netting, and irrigation tubing were used to maintain a climatic "cooling effect" throughout the courtyard. Oscillating fans mounted on a concrete wall generated varying "wind conditions"; atomizers secured overhead distributed a fine mist; and flexible screens of iridescent fabric produced areas of shade and privacy. Twelve pivoting nylon hammocks supported by steel columns and three fifteen-foot circular blue pools offered therapeutic activities. Portable "hydration packs," hung like intravenous drips above the hammocks, provided a refreshing source of drinking water. Surreal yet suggestive of existing urban conditions, the cumulative effect of these devices provoked visual tension and disorientation in an otherwise spa-like environment.

Installation view
Opposite page, from left: detail
of elevation; plan climate diagram

cancer alley
mississippi river, louisiana
2001–

This project, a collaboration with the photographer Richard Misrach, is part of a larger intervention reclaiming key sites along "Cancer Alley," a toxic eighty-mile stretch of the Mississippi River between Baton Rouge and New Orleans. Here majestic antebellum plantation homes remain as icons of a bygone era, side by side with the looming petrochemical plants, refineries, and grain elevators that are their contemporary counterparts.

Roy's proposal addresses a landscape and community in crisis through the programming and implementation of a flexible, modular system of retrofitted industrial river barges. Requiring modest investment and no extensive land purchases, these large floating platforms—both temporary and permanent—can be grouped together to accommodate a variety of activities and form a continually reconfigurable "landscape." Depending on their intended functions, the barges may be used to provide local residents with libraries, computer labs, sports facilities, and floating gardens, each meant to augment the area's impoverished infrastructure and contaminated environment. These community-oriented barges would operate on a timetable to serve the local parishes. Roy's scheme also encompasses a series of mobile riverfront developments that include motels, parking, cafés, landscaped parks, and drive-in movie theaters—modern-day showboats intended to attract tourists and stimulate additional improvements throughout the region.

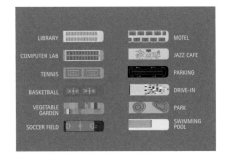 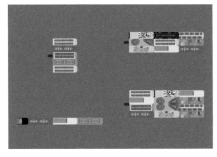

Proposed barge programs and possible configurations Opposite page, from top: conceptual views of motel and drive-in theater. Photographic material courtesy of Richard Misrach

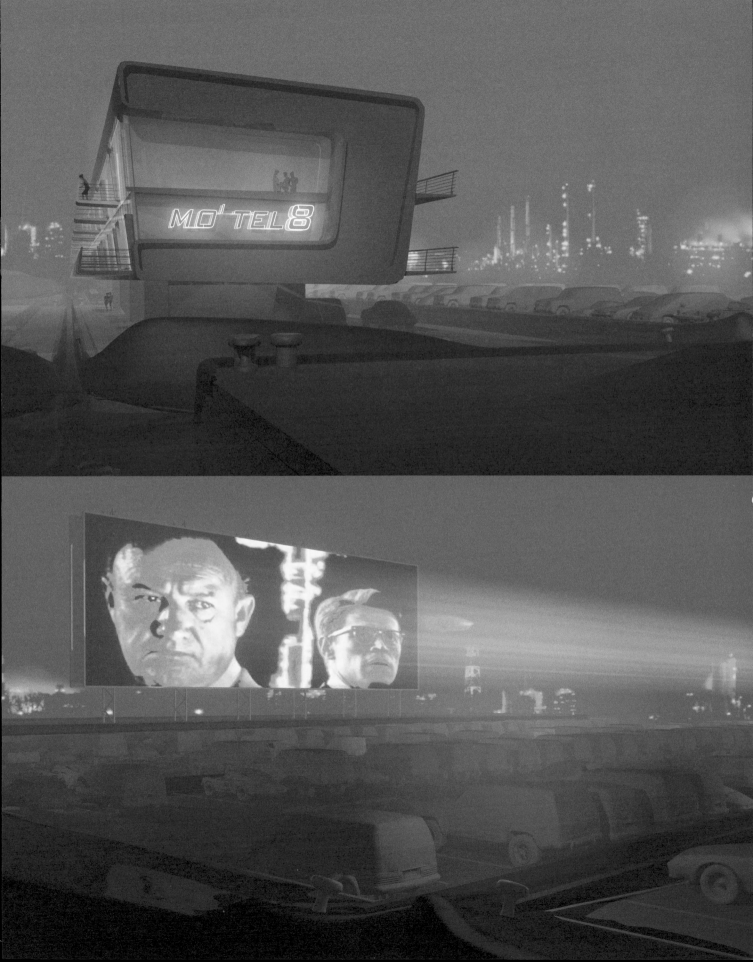

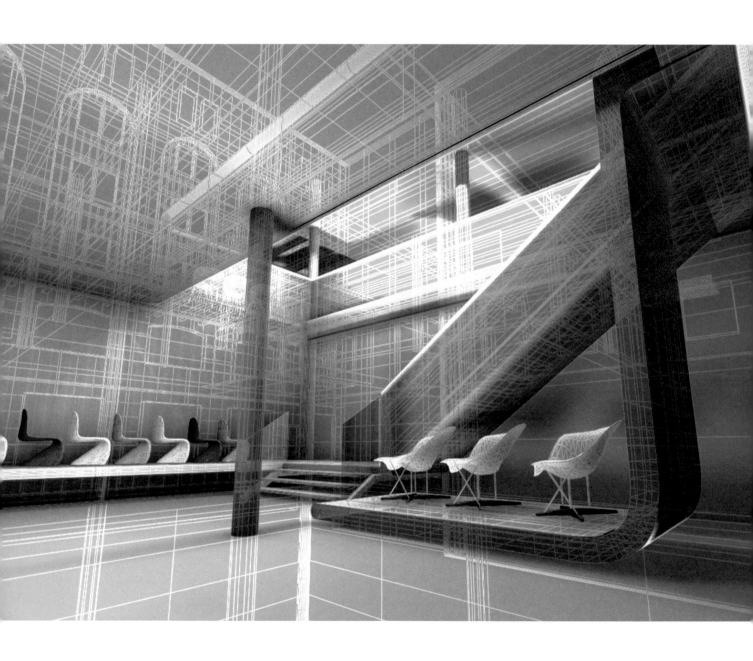

Wire-frame rendering of first-floor retail area
Opposite page: conceptual section diagrams

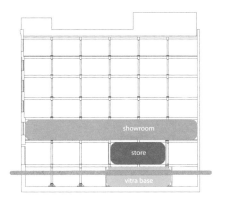
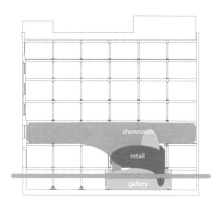

vitra
new york
2001–2002

Vitra, the distinguished Swiss furniture manufacturer, recently chose New York's Meatpacking District as the location for its new 13,000-square-foot showroom—three floors tucked within a six-story, loft-style warehouse. Roy's first realized commercial commission, the design performs a series of interventions to the original structure, transforming the existing space into an environment that weaves together a variety of client needs: offices, retail, gallery, and showroom.

The public face of the showroom, a glass entry and adjacent window display spanning the width of the interior, is divided by a rectangular signage wall. Just inside the outer wall, a triple-height "slot" allows natural light to penetrate the interior and basement of the once-dark industrial building. This atriumlike space is one of two multistory openings created by removing portions of the existing concrete slabs. The slots accommodate bridges, balconies, and glass balustrades that create a dynamic interplay between the three floors.

The gallery, located on the basement level, is reached by descending a staircase just inside the entrance. A platform bridging the void created by the three-story opening leads to the slightly raised first-floor retail area. The offices and showroom on the top floor are accessed via a staircase inserted into a double-height slot at the rear of the retail level. Placing circulation at the front and back of the space allows for an open plan at the center, maximizing capacity on the sales floor.

Roy's spatial solution reworks the original building's simple layout, seamlessly integrating program and structure. Additional consolidation of the three floors is accomplished through the use of large, gray "tongues" for display surfaces. Running like catwalks from the second-floor showroom to the retail and gallery levels below, these rubber-wrapped forms add sculptural detail to the overall scheme.

From top: view of showroom street entrance; first-floor retail area; triple-height slot at entrance; retail level
Opposite page: sections

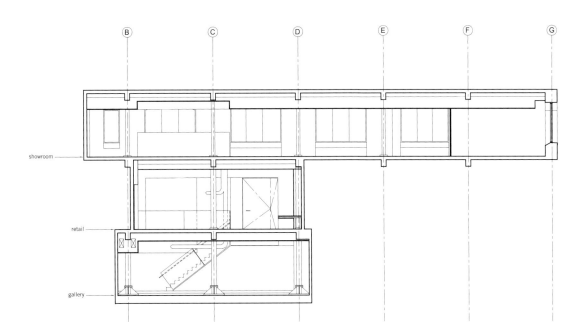

showroom

retail

gallery

B   C   D   E   F   G

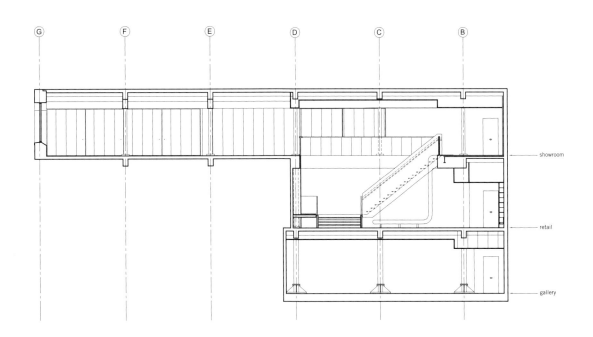

G   F   E   D   C   B

showroom

retail

gallery

From top: aerial view; perspective
Opposite page: north-facing elevation

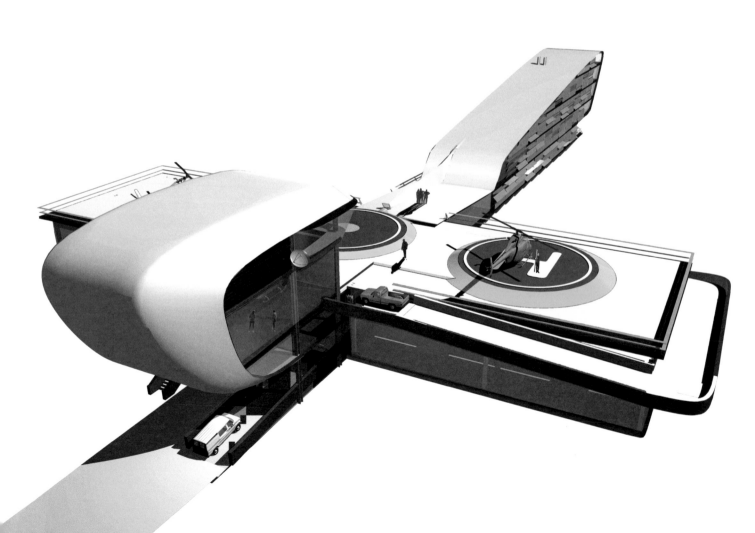

wind river lodge
chugach mountain range, alaska
2001–

Designed for Alaska Rendezvous Heli-ski Guides, the Wind River Lodge stands in southern Alaska's Chugach mountain range, a dramatic environment of inaccessible glacial ridges and peaks, some rising nearly nine thousand feet. Serving as the base for an extreme skiing operation, this 52,000-square-foot complex comprises a hotel, heliport and control tower, bar, enclosed maintenance hangar, and warehouse spaces.

Emerging from the landscape like a tanker trapped in the ice, the compound is defined by a continuous surface that wraps around a steel frame to form floors, walls, and ceilings capable of bearing the weight of heavy snow. A series of concrete "fins" support the building, ensuring that it sits above the snow line. The twenty-six-room lodge, identified by its large, low-sloping roof, is economically designed as a cluster of prefabricated units. Built and then shipped to the site, the modular rooms are slotted into the hotel's folding structure. The lodge's south-facing elevation is sheathed in a series of galvanized sheet-metal louvers that provide solar protection as well as an appealingly varied surface. The northwest facade, made entirely of glass, reflects the majestic landscape beyond.

An indoor passage below the rectangular helipad deck connects the hotel to the heliport. An elevated tower, oriented just south of the helipad to avoid collisions, contains an enclosed maintenance hangar and a large warehouse used for storing off-season equipment. The top-floor air traffic control room and adjacent bar frame panoramic views of the natural surroundings through a large, overhanging window. Here skiers can relax in a luxurious atmosphere and relive the day's adventures.

Despite its severe natural context and the high-tech activities it accommodates, the Wind River Lodge introduces a certain elegance to the perilous sport of heliskiing. Seeking to embody its patrons' spirit of adventure, the lodge harnesses the drama of light, landscape, and sensory stimulation to create the ultimate alpine experience.

Side perspective of south-facing elevation
Opposite page, from left: second-floor plan;
ground-floor plan

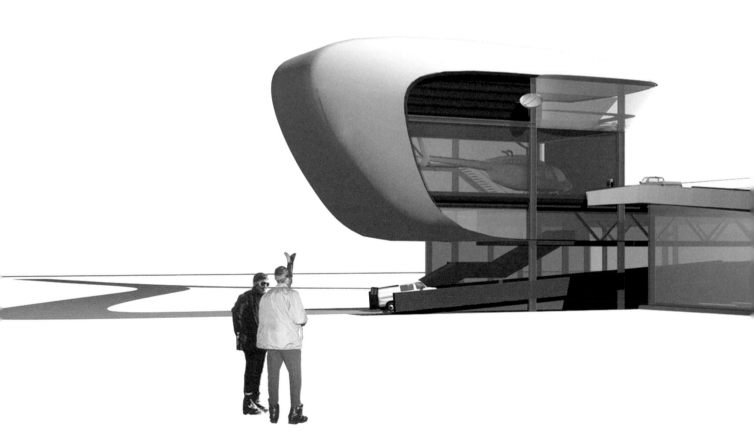

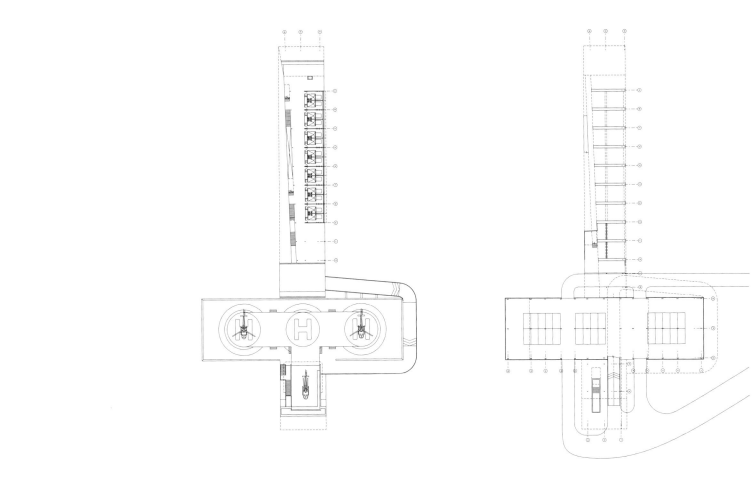
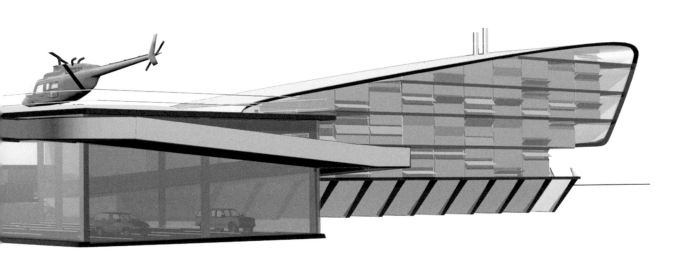

project information

Projects highlighted in orange are represented in the exhibition *ROY/design series 1*.

Okavango Delta Spa

Location: Okavango River Delta, Botswana
Design: 1997–
Status: schematic design
Size: 11.5-acre site
Principal structural system: wood frame
Principal materials: wood, thatch, fiberglass, aluminum, and nylon fabric
Client: Uncharted Africa
Design team: Lindy Roy with Albert Angel, Gavin Bardes, Karen Bullis, Aline Cautis, Heidi McDowell, Ana Miljacki, Lee Moreau, John Mueller, Chris Perry, and Mary Springer

VHouse

Location: Houston
Design: 1999–
Status: construction documents
Size: 1,450 square feet
Principal structural system: wood frame
Principal materials: galvanized sheet metal, Viroc, glass, and wood
Client: Fifth Ward Community Redevelopment Corporation
Design team: Lindy Roy with Mark Kroeckel (Openshop/Studio) and Albert Angel, Karen Bullis, Chris Perry, Eric Schultz, and Paul Stewart

Issey Miyake

Location: New York
Design: 2000
Status: invited competition proposal
Size: 9,000 square feet
Principal structural system: N/A
Principal materials: steel, concrete, optical fiber, and wood
Client: Issey Miyake USA
Design team: Lindy Roy with Albert Angel and Anthony Burke

Poolhouse

Location: Sagaponac, New York
Design: 2000–
Status: construction documents
Size: 3,400 square feet
Principal structural system: steel frame
Principal materials: steel, glass, wood, and concrete
Client: The Brown Companies
Design team: Lindy Roy with Mark Kroeckel (Openshop/Studio), Jason Lee, Barbara Ludescher, Gernot Riether, Monica Tiulescu, and Louise Vrou
Structural engineer: Robert Silman Associates, P.C.
Mechanical engineer: Székely Engineering

Noah

Location: New York
Design: 2001–
Status: schematic design
Size: 2,200 square feet
Principal structural system: N/A
Principal materials: steel, concrete, optical fiber, cast resin, and leather
Client: undisclosed
Design team: Lindy Roy with Jonus Coersmeier, Tracy Geraldez, Michael Maggio, Monica Tiulescu, and Heidi Werner

subWave

Location: P.S.1 Contemporary Art Center, Long Island City, New York
Design: 2001
Construction: 2001

Status: competition proposal for the Museum of
Modern Art/P.S.1 Young Architects Program;
awarded March 2001; completed June 2001;
disassembled September 2001
Size: 2,200 square feet
Principal structural system: steel frame
Principal materials: steel, canvas, netting, steel cable,
irrigation hosing, and nozzles
Client: The Museum of Modern Art, New York,
and P.S.1 Contemporary Art Center
Design team: Lindy Roy with Benjamin Aranda
and Barbara Ludscher, Philip Kelly, Tomoyuki
Minowa, Gernot Riether, and Monica Tiulescu
Installation team: Albert Angel, Rebecca Arcaro,
Andrew Ballard, Katherine Chang, Hayley Eber, Pablo
Garcia, Jorge Godoy, Till Houtermans, Fuki Ikeda,
Chris Lasch, Mariam Mojdehi, Anna Niemark, Ayako
Ohkawa, Wade Perrin, Roberto Steck-Ibarra, Itsuka
Sugimoto, Akiko Watanabe, and Joshuah Webster
Contractor: The Oculus Group Ltd. and
Cabezon Design Group
Structural engineer: Dewhurst MacFarlane and
Partners Inc.

Cancer Alley

Location: Mississippi River, Louisiana
Design: 2001–
Status: schematic design
Size: eighty-mile site
Structural system: N/A
Materials: N/A
Client: N/A
Collaboration with Richard Misrach
Design team: Lindy Roy with Albert Angel,
Pomdet Chandamanich, Yolanda do Campo,
Barbara Ludescher, and J. Christopher Whitelaw

Vitra

Location: New York
Design: 2001
Construction: 2002

Status: completed
Size: 13,000 square feet
Principal structural system: steel and wood frame
Principal materials: steel, wood, rubber, and
polycarbonate panels
Client: Vitra USA
Design team: Lindy Roy with Mark Kroeckel
(Openshop/Studio), Sandra Donough, Tracy
Geraldez, Jason Lee, Barbara Ludescher, Gernot
Riether, and Heidi Werner
Architect of record: Peter Himmelstein Design
Contractor: Vanguard Construction and
Development Co. Inc.
Structural engineer: Anchor Consulting
Mechanical engineer: Stanislav Slutsky,
P.E. Consulting Engineers
Graphic design: 2x4

Wind River Lodge

Location: Chugach mountain range, Alaska
Design: 2001–
Status: schematic design
Size: 52,000 square feet
Principal structural system: steel frame and
prefabricated concrete panels
Principal materials: steel, concrete, galvanized
sheet metal, wood, stone, and glass
Client: Alaska Rendezvous Heli-ski Guides
Design team: Lindy Roy with Gavin Bardes,
Jason Lee, and Michael Maggio

selected
bibliography

Albrecht, Donald, with Elizabeth Johnson.
New Hotels for Global Nomads. New York:
Merrell and Cooper-Hewitt, National Design Museum, 2002.

Brown, Mark. "Practice Q&A."
I.D. 49, no. 3 (May 2002): 84–85.

Czarnecki, John E. "Taking a Leap of Faith."
Architectural Record 190, no. 12 (December 2002): 73–80.

Iovine, Julie V. "An Architect Finds Her Buzz."
New York Times, 14 November 2002.

Kwinter, Sanford. "African Genesis."
Assemblage 36 (August 1998): 24–41.

Muschamp, Herbert. "A spa that lets
the buildings take a dip, too."
New York Times, 23 March 1997.

——. "Thinking Big: A Plan for Ground Zero and Beyond."
New York Times Magazine, 8 September 2002.

Nobel, Philip. "The Twin Towers."
Vogue 191, no. 9 (September 2001): 466–70.

Poels, Jan-Willem. "A Meaty Experience."
Frame 22 (September/October 2001): 82–85.

Renzi, Jen. "Extreme Measures."
Interior Design (November 2001): 138–41.

Roy, Lindy. "Coordination: African Delta Spa."
Assemblage 36 (August 1998): 42–63.

Sinnott, Abby. "Out of Site."
One 2, no. 4 (August/September 2001): 45–46.